Beginning Fiddle

By Stacy Phillips

Exclusive Distributors:
Music Sales Corporation
257 Park Avenue South, New York, NY 10010 USA
Music Sales Limited
8/9 Frith Street, London W1V 5TZ England
Music Sales Pty. Limited
120 Rothschild Street, Rosebery, Sydney, NSW 2018, Australia

Copyright © 1990 by Amsco Publications
Order No. AM 71275
US ISBN 978.0.8256.2541.1
UK ISBN 0.7119.1497.4

Printed in the United States of America by
Vicks Lithograph and Printing Corporation

Music Sales America

DISTRIBUTED BY

HAL•LEONARD®
CORPORATION

7777 W. BLUEMOUND RD. P.O. BOX 13819 MILWAUKEE, WI 53213

Contents

Introduction

The instructions that follow are designed to get you started playing traditional fiddle music. Each musical example in the book features a melody line which illustrates how fiddle technique is applied in a particular context.

For novices to music notation, some introductory material on this subject is supplied in the Appendix. If you encounter an unfamiliar symbol or term in the course of the book, refer to this section for its definition. Symbols and expressions that are not defined in the Appendix are explained as they appear in the text.

There is no difference between a violin and a fiddle. Although these two terms have different derivations, they refer to one and the same instrument. So, slip this book into your instrument case, hike to a secluded glade, abandoned tenement, or the comfort of your room at home, and begin to fiddle away to your heart's content.

Getting Started

There is no single, correct way to hold a fiddle and a bow, although the illustrations in this book should give you an idea of the variety of grips that are practical. If a method works for you, there is no need to conform to some putative norm. Just go with it.

Here are some general guidelines regarding grip. Keep both wrists limp. Tight wrists keep the noting fingers from working efficiently, and prevent you from changing bow direction smoothly. If you decide to hold your violin against your shoulder (as opposed to your chest), hold it firmly between the left side of your lower jaw (not the point of your chin) and the inside of your left shoulder (not the top). Grip the instrument firmly between your shoulder and jaw. In this way, your noting hand is free to work the fingerboard.

You can hold the violin beneath your chin without any support from your noting hand.

One advantage of holding the violin against your chest is that you can play and sing—or even call a square dance—at the same time.

Here, the violin is held against the player's chest.

No matter which method you use to support the fiddle, don't let the neck rest in the hollow between your thumb and forefinger.

The strings of the violin are tuned to E, A, D, G, respectively—beginning with the first, or highest, string and ending with the fourth, or lowest, string. You can tune to another instrument, or you may use a pitch pipe or an electronic tuner to accomplish the task. At first, you may feel that it takes an absurdly long time to get the strings in tune, but after a week or two, it should take only a couple minutes. Make an extra effort to tune out the last bit of dissonance before beginning to play.

The strings are tuned an interval of a fifth apart. Thus, there are five scale steps between the E string and the A string—counting E as 1, D as 2, C as 3, B as 4, and A as 5. Similarly, five scale steps occur between the second and third strings—from A to D—as well as between the third and fourth strings—D to G. You will eventually learn to recognize the sound of this interval, and tune by ear.

Let's take a look at the violin bow and its components.

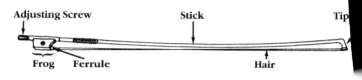

The violin bow

Some fiddlers hold the bow with the thumb in the space between the *frog* and the *stick,* with the fingers splayed on top of the stick.

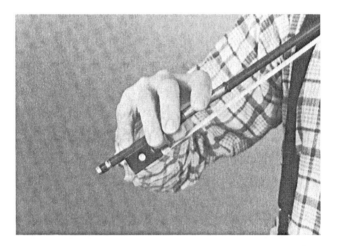

Standard bow grip

Some players place their thumbs beneath the frog.

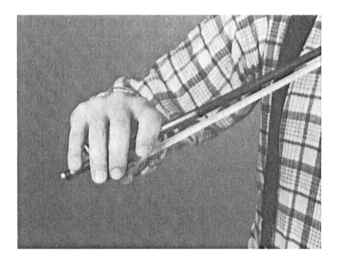

Alternate bow grip, with the thumb beneath the frog

The hair of your bow should be tightened so that it does not touch the stick when you are playing. Always relax the hair pressure when you are not playing. The hair of a bow must be kept sticky with rosin, so that it catches on the strings. Without the rosin, the hair glides over the strings, and no tone is produced.

Grab the bow and try playing some notes. You may either push the bow in an upstroke (denoted as ∨), or pull the bow in a downstroke (denoted as ⊓). Use the entire length of the stick as you play each tone in the example below. Make sure that you hit only one string at a time.

Now play the same example with reverse bowing—that is, substituting upstrokes for downstrokes, and vice versa.

The bow should be placed at an approximate midpoint between the bridge and the end of the fingerboard, and moved at a perpendicular angle to the strings. In fact, the bow should stay at a right angle to the strings for the entire length of the bowstroke. The fiddle's tone changes according to bow placement. Some players like to place the bow a bit closer to the bridge, while others prefer it nearer to the fingerboard. Try to keep the bow from slipping up or down the strings during a bowstroke.

Let your elbow, wrist, and fingers do the work. Keep your shoulder relaxed, and don't jerk it around. Bow movement is mainly provided by the arm from the elbow down, so try not to keep that joint stiff. Let's look at the wrist's position at the beginning of a bowstroke.

The wrist at the beginning of a bowstroke

Now, here is how the wrist looks at the end of a bowstroke.

The wrist at the end of a bowstroke

Your wrist should start to change direction just before the bow direction changes. The smooth execution of this wrist movement will help you to avoid making a choppy sound with each new stroke of the bow. Of course, a smooth change is not always desirable, as you will discover when the accent in a single shuffle pattern is later discussed.

Before you begin learning scales and fingerings, take a look at the violin and its components.

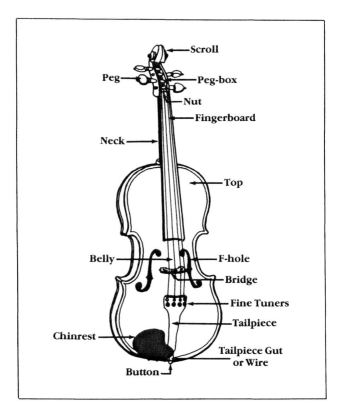

The violin and its components

The key of A is easiest to start with. The spacing of your fingers for an A scale on the A (second) and E (first) strings is shown in the accompanying illustrations. The dots on the diagram indicate where you should place the center of each fingerpad. The large spaces between the dots indicate *whole steps,* and the small spaces indicate *half steps.* A combination of whole steps and half steps is needed to create a major scale. Now, try the finger spacing for the A scale, as shown.

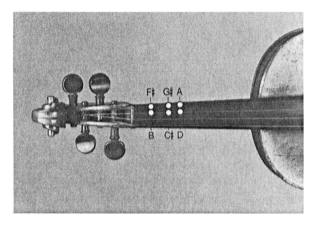

Finger Spacing Pattern One

The numbers in the following A scale refer to the fingers that should stop the indicated notes: 0 = open string, 1 = index finger, 2 = middle finger, 3 = ring finger, and 4 = pinky. You will not need the pinky for this exercise, although it will be used later in the book. Start the scale with a downstroke.

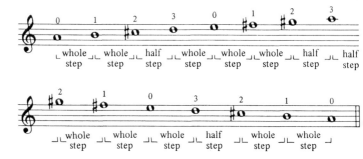

When you place the second finger down, keep the first down as well. When you play the D note, the first and second fingers should remain down. In order to minimize motion, try to keep any unused fingers hovering over the area in which they will be soon needed. (By the way, it is necessary to keep your fingernails short in order to prevent them from gouging the wood of the fingerboard.)

Practice the A scale until your fingers automatically fall into the correct spacings. Most accomplished players do not need to focus on their fingers. Through practice, they have developed an instinctive knowledge of pitch fingerings.

The C, F, and G notes are always sharped in an A major scale. This information is notated at the beginning of each staff in the *key signature*. Try playing this scale variation in the key of A.

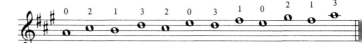

Now, try this descending variation.

Facility with these permutations of basic scales is very important because many tunes incorporate these patterns.

It's time to try your hand at a complete tune in the key of A. "On Top of Old Smokey" is a familiar favorite with a full octave range. Play one bowstroke per note, and make sure to hold each note for its full duration. There are three beats in each measure.

You can expect some squawks to occur as you play this tune the first few times. These are usually the result of too much bow pressure, or a stray finger touching a bowed string.

On Top of Old Smokey (Key of A)

Refer to the Appendix if you are unsure of the meaning of some of the symbols in the notation of "On Top of Old Smokey." The three notes before the double barline are introductory notes which form a *lead-in,* or *pickup.* The F♯ note that starts off the second measure is held for five beats: three beats are denoted by the dotted half note, and two more are indicated by the half note in the next measure. These two notes are attached with a curved line called a *tie.* The E note that occurs two measures later is held for eight beats: that is, two dotted half notes (six beats), tied to one more half note (or two beats). Play these continuously with a single bowstroke.

At first, you may have a tendency to move the bow faster than needed. As a result, you may run out of hair before eight beats are counted. Gaining the control to slow the speed of your bowstroke, and eventually increasing the tempo of this piece, will solve this problem.

The Single Shuffle

When starting to play the fiddle, you may concentrate more on the correct placement of your fingers than good bowing technique. Contrary to what you might expect, bowing is central to good fiddling. To illustrate this fact, first try playing the basic melody of the whimsically titled "Boil the Cabbage Down."

Boil the Cabbage Down

This somewhat drab melody may be made positively zesty with some bowing variations. The most common bowing pattern is a repeating cycle of long-short-short strokes. On the open A string, this cycle might occur as follows.

This pattern is called the *single shuffle*. Notice how the long bow alternates between a downstroke and an upstroke. The single shuffle pattern gives "Boil the Cabbage Down" a traditional fiddle sound.

Boil the Cabbage Down (With a Single Shuffle)

The key to getting a good single shuffle feel is to accent the first short stroke of each cycle. You can do this by increasing your finger pressure on the bow, or by suddenly moving it faster on the accented beat. The prominence of this accent may vary according to taste and content—from a barely discernible volume increase to a sharp snap. Here is the single shuffle pattern, with marked accents.

As you increase the tempo, the accent pattern will sound more natural and propulsive. You will find that fiddle tunes with many short notes (like some of the *breakdowns* in this book), should be played using the middle third of the bow (or less). Some styles of old-time playing require only a couple of inches of bow per stroke. This type of playing used to be referred to as *jiggy bow* fiddling. When playing in this traditional style, fiddlers like to choke up on the bow; that is, they hold the bow at a point high up the length of the stick.

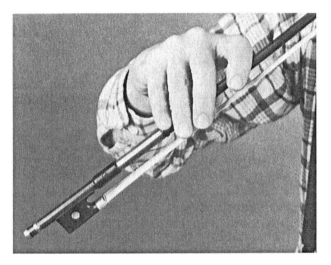

Choking up on the bow

As you move the bow more quickly, it naturally causes the strings to emit a distinctly different sound. During fast passages, you should use the middle of the bow. Your wrist should do almost all the work, while your forearm moves only a bit. For this reason, your wrist must remain relaxed and supple.

If, at this point, you are having trouble staying in tune, try any or all of the following:

• Occasionally check your tuning. Hard playing, temperature variations, and humidity can change the tension in strings. Make sure that your tuning pegs are holding firmly.

• Keep your fingers hovering just above the required finger spacing. Because your hand is probably not used to stretching, you may find that as you reach for one note, you will pull another finger sharp or flat. You may need to exercise your hand for a few minutes each day by gently stretching apart your fingers, so that their reach increases.

• If you grip the neck of the violin with your thumb, it can limit the quick stretching of your noting fingers. This is why both wrists must remain loose. Your chin and shoulder should support the instrument.

• Make sure that you press the strings down firmly.

The only things missing from a complete rendition of "Boil the Cabbage Down," are a kickoff and a tag. The *kickoff* is designed to set the tempo for your fellow musicians, and give them sufficient time to gird their musical loins. The typical fiddle kickoff uses the form known colloquially as *potatoes* (perhaps, more accurately, *taters*). This traditional kickoff is usually eight beats in length (though it is sometimes extended to sixteen beats).

Remember the accents as you play the following single shuffle kickoff to "Boil the Cabbage Down."

One ta-ter, two ta-ter, three ta-ter, four ta-ter.

Any kickoff should be arranged so that the first note of the tune proper (that is, the first note after the double barline) is bowed with a downstroke.

Tags make ensemble members aware of the imminent ending of a tune. They are not as formalized as kickoffs, but usually last for eight beats. The familiar "shave-and-a-haircut-two-bits" song ending is a stock example of a tag. With "Boil the Cabbage Down," the following tag may be added after the last measure of the final statement of the melody. This next example shows the last two measures of the tune, leading in to an effective tag. Give this one a try.

This tag may also be played with a shuffle rhythm, but here, two notes are played during the long bowstroke. A curved line that links notes of different pitches is known as a *slur*. This indicates that bow direction should not change for any of the indicated notes. Try playing the tag again, with this in mind.

Now that you know the kickoff and tag for "Boil the Cabbage Down," try playing the whole arrangement in tempo. Take the time to memorize this sequence.

The Key of D

As you know, the interval between each adjacent fiddle string is the same. This means that you may use the finger spacing for the A scale (Finger Spacing Pattern One) to create a scale in the key of D. To accomplish this, simply begin the scale pattern on the D string.

Once you are familiar with this scale, try playing "On Top of Old Smokey" in the key of D. Note that the new key signature contains F♯ and C♯.

On Top of Old Smokey (Key of D)

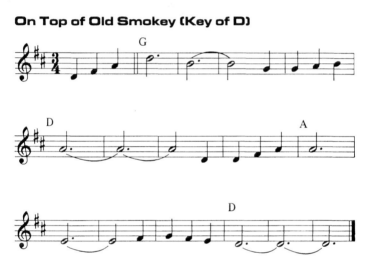

You should also be familiar with the upward extension of the D scale on the E string. A different finger spacing is necessary to accomplish this (Finger Spacing Pattern Two).

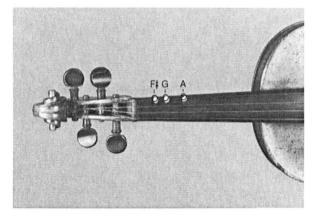

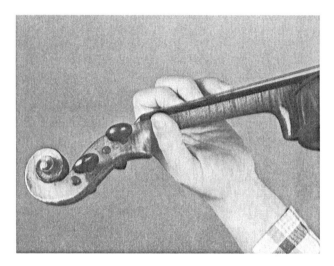

Finger Spacing Pattern Two

In music notation, this extension would appear as follows.

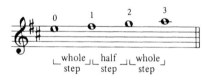

You will need to use the first three strings of your instrument to play "Mississippi Sawyer." Notice the use of the single shuffle pattern, especially in the first section. Remember to accent the first short stroke of each shuffle sequence.

Mississippi Sawyer

This arrangement of "Mississippi Sawyer" exhibits a typical fiddle-tune form—that is, two repeated sections. The first section is played and then repeated before going on to the second section, which is also repeated once.

You can use four potatoes for a kickoff.

Try ending "Mississippi Sawyer" with a tag similar to the one used in "Boil the Cabbage Down."

"Mississippi Sawyer" introduces another basic fiddling technique called *rocking the bow*. As illustrated in the first measure of the second section of the tune, this entails the use of alternating strings in a note series. Practice this technique using the open A and E strings.

The rocking action of this technique becomes more evident when notes go by a bit faster. Try this technique in the next tune, "Harvest Home Hornpipe," in which rocking is fundamental to the melody.

Harvest Home Hornpipe

This Scottish/Irish tune uses all *saw strokes* (that is, one note per bow). British tunes do not usually use kickoffs and tags, although these conventions do work well with many of these tunes.

The Key of G

To form a G scale, simply move the D scale down to the G and D strings, and apply Finger Spacing Pattern One. The low strings lend this scale a relatively dark, rich texture.

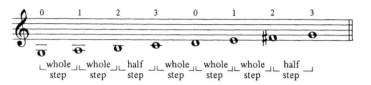

As with the D scale, Finger Spacing Pattern Two will here allow you to extend the G scale upward. Try extending this scale up another whole octave, plus one note. Note that the key signature of G contains only an F sharp. Start this extended scale with the last note of the G scale.

Here's a rather lengthy scale variation in the key of G. To make things more interesting, your pinky is now called to action. The notes played with the fourth finger should match the open string directly above. In fact, you may periodically compare the tone of the open string with the note played by the fourth finger to make sure that the stopped note is in tune.

Generally, the fourth finger is used instead of an open string for one of the following reasons:

• To slide up or down to a note.

• To make it possible to apply *vibrato* to a note.

• To avoid a potentially awkward bowing.

The single shuffle phrase that follows illustrates the use of the fourth finger where the open string would require an awkward bowing. Play this short phrase, as shown.

Clearly, it is easier to finger the A note than to switch strings (without changing bow direction). The fourth finger must also be used in this way for scales that include no open strings.

"Muddy Roads" employs all four strings of the violin. The first section is in the key of G, and the second section is in D. This change in key signature during the song is called a *modulation.* At this point in the song, C notes become sharped, so be aware of your finger spacings. Count four potatoes and play this one.

Muddy Roads

Slides and Blues

Now let's add one of the fiddler's favorite ornaments—the *slide* (or *glissando,* as it is more formally called). This is an easy maneuver that can add much expression to your playing. The blues is a typical setting for this effect. The basic blues is twelve *bars* (or measures) in length. In this style, the third and seventh notes of a scale are often flatted. Thus, in the key of G, the B and F♯ notes would become B♭ and F, respectively.

In the G blues that follows, the diagonal arrows symbolize a quick slide (about a half step in length) up to the indicated note. Because the tone at the beginning of the slide is not held at all, it is not notated in the example. Start each slide immediately, and move quickly to the notated tone. Play this blues slowly, and bow it any way you wish.

Blues in G

The G♯ note in the ninth measure of this tune is one half step below the A note that follows. The last seven notes form a typical blues tag. As you are dealing with quite a few accidentals in this piece, proper finger placement becomes important.

"Florida Blues" follows a typical blues form, but it is usually played up-tempo. When you encounter two consecutive slides (as in the first measure), you will need to move your fingers pretty quickly. Be sure to stop the bow between the two upward slides, so no downward glissando is discernible between them.

The B♯ note in measure nine is equivalent to a C note, and the E♯ in the eleventh measure is the same as F. The jagged symbol in measure eleven indicates a slide of definite length (here F♯ to E♯, or one half-step). Hold each note for the duration of one eighth-note. Give this tune a try.

Florida Blues

As an experiment, turn back now to "Harvest Home Hornpipe" and try to slide into the F♯ in the first measure. This will give you an idea of how this device sounds in a non-blues setting.

The Key of C

The first note of the scale in the key of C is played with the third finger on the fourth string. Finger Spacing Pattern Two is then employed as the scale continues up through the D and A strings. Here is the portion of the scale played on the D string.

Here is the portion of the C scale played on the A string. (Notice that the key of C has no sharps or flats.)

Let's play "On Top of Old Smokey" again to get accustomed to this new scale.

On Top of Old Smokey (Key of C)

When playing this scale below the C note, return to Finger Spacing Pattern One. Extending the scale up to the E string requires a new spacing pattern.

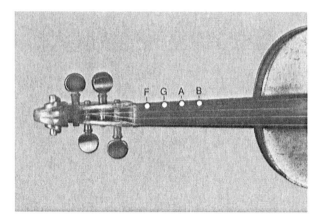

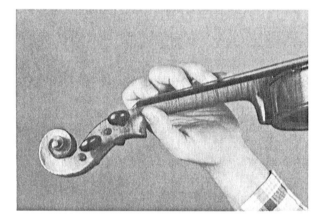

Finger Spacing Pattern Three

Here is an extended variation of the C scale, with indicated finger spacing patterns.

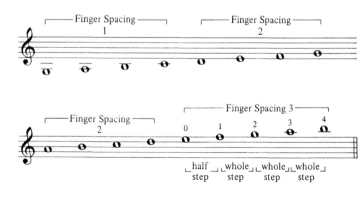

The last few notes of this example require the biggest stretch yet for your fingers. Your first finger will probably need to be raised off the string when your fourth finger stops the B note. Try to keep the other fingers down. Some people with large hands can even extend the pinky up another half step to a high C.

"Back Up and Push" begins with a slide for the fourth finger. The first three notes form the pickup.

Back Up and Push

You will need to use some pretty long bowstrokes to play the notes that are held for four beats or more. As you practice moving the bow at different speeds, you will notice that you are able to move it quite slowly and still produce a pleasing tone. As you play this tune, make sure to hold each note for its full duration. An A note occurs on the third beat of the first measure, and is held through the first beat of the second measure (a duration of three beats).

You may want to start this tune off with the standard potatoes kickoff. If so, use one measure of "taters" instead of two, as shown.

To provide contrast to the long bowstrokes of "Back Up and Push," fiddlers often add a shuffle section to the arrangement. Try this shuffle variation slowly at first. Remember to change your finger placement when you play on the E string. You'll find that this variation is a good exercise to practice for the development of your dexterity and playing speed. The first two measures of this variation form an alternate second ending for the previous version. Here, a different three-beat pickup is played to introduce the shuffle variation.

Back Up and Push (With Single Shuffle)

Double Stops

Double stops are created when the bow rubs against two adjacent strings, and two notes are played simultaneously. Double stops provide a nice touch when added to the basic melody of "Back Up and Push." Try playing the open E string as the fourth finger slides up to an E note. The two strings, sounding together, add a biting accent to the beginning of the tune. (This is also a good time to check that the pinky note is in tune.) The sharp sound of the slide is dissonant at first, then blends consonantly with the E note. The sounding of two identical notes is a typical occurrence in traditional Southern fiddle music. When the two notes are truly in tune, they sound like one loud note. Here's the pickup.

The zero in the notation means that the E string is open. The numeral four indicates that the A string is fingered with the pinky. If you get a squeaking noise when you try this double stop, you are probably allowing your pinky to graze the E string.

"Boil the Cabbage Down" is a prime subject for some easy double stops. Run over the basic melody once again, then try it with double stops, as shown.

Boil the Cabbage Down (With Double Stops)

This arrangement affords many opportunities for unwanted squeaks, so take it slowly and keep your wrists loose. Note the F♯ over the D note in the second measure. Play each note of the piece in tune separately before trying the double stops. It will probably take a little practice before you are able to go from measure to measure without hesitation.

In the notation of the double-stop version of "Muddy Roads" that follows, the open string drones are separated from the melody notes, wherever possible. This unclutters the staff a bit.

Muddy Roads (With Double Stops)

In this tune, the open string drones occur both above and below the melody. In the eighth measure, a D note on the A string forms a double stop with the open E. This has a somewhat dissonant effect, but is nevertheless acceptable because it passes so quickly.

As you play the double stops, make the bow pressure equal on both strings to assure equal volume for equal notes.

Double stops are among the most challenging of fiddling techniques. As you experiment with them, you will find that all sorts of note combinations are possible. Keep in mind that a given melody note may be used as the high or low note of a double stop. Make sure each note of a double stop is in tune before playing the two notes in concert.

Try playing the double stops illustrated below. Note that in each one there's a half-step spacing between the two fingers. Since they are on different strings, the difference in pitch is a sixth.

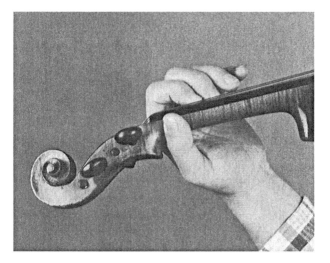

Playing a double stop

The three double stops that follow are similar to the one played in "Boil the Cabbage Down."

Here are two sets of double stops, each of which works well as a potato kickoff. Try beginning "Muddy Roads" with either of these kickoffs.

A kickoff with double stops also works well with "Mississippi Sawyer."

Here's another good double-stop kickoff for "Mississippi Saw-yer."

Let's look at a few one-finger double stops. Here, the same finger must stop both strings. When you play these, you must keep the finger absolutely perpendicular to the strings in order to keep both notes in tune. This variety of double stop may be tricky at first.

Turn back to "Blues in G" and play it again with these double stops added in measure seven.

Sliding into double stops in this way can really be effective.

Finger Spacing
Pattern Four

Extending the A scale down an octave onto the D and G strings requires a fourth pattern of finger spacing.

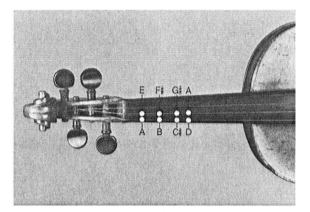

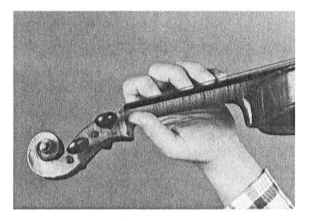

Finger Spacing Pattern Four

Beginning on the G string, the extended scale is as follows.

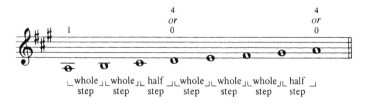

Combine this series with the A scale you have learned previously to form a two-octave scale.

"Growling Old Man and Growling Old Woman" is a challenging tune that alternates between a G scale and an A scale. (Remember that the key of G requires Finger Spacing Pattern One on the two low strings and Finger Spacing Pattern Two on the two high strings.) This tune kicks off with a one-finger double stop. The tag features a rhythmic figure on the same double stop.

Growling Old Man and Growling Old Woman

By the way, the low part of this tune's melody is meant to represent the old man, while the high-pitched section brings to mind his female counterpart. Remember to emphasize the accents in this single shuffle pattern.

Finger Spacing Pattern Four is also used on the A string when playing in the key of D, as in "Arkansas Traveller." Try this tune out for yourself.

Arkansas Traveller

Facts and Fancy About Fiddle Hardware

These days, a functional, gently-used student violin can still be had for a reasonable price. On the high end of the scale, there are violins that are worth a small fortune. Whatever type you choose, make sure it suits your needs. Some violins are not sturdy enough to take to music festivals and play outdoors. They need to be treated like spoiled children. However, if you are going to play it in the home or studio, a fiddle's stamina in this area need not be a primary issue.

Be sure to check that the tuning pegs of an instrument do not slip, and that there are no cracks, especially along the violin's seams. Also, make sure the bridge of an instrument remains perpendicular to the body, especially after thorough tuning.

Strings are available in metal, perlon, or any number of other materials. Some experimentation is necessary in order to establish your preference. The metal strings are a bit louder and easier to tune. However, their sound is somewhat harsh, and they create a good deal of tension on the body of the instrument. Some strings may be tuned with the aid of fine tuners. These tuners may be bought separately or are included as part of a *tailpiece*. However, fine tuners will not function with gut strings.

A good set of strings is surprisingly expensive—but quality strings will make up for their cost by lasting a long time, especially if they are made of metal. As strings get worn, they become difficult to tune, and there is a distinct loss of volume and tone. If the winding of a string becomes undone, it's time to spring for a new set of four.

Some players prefer to use a shoulder rest clamped under the bottom of the violin. This accessory can make it easier to grip the fiddle without the use of your noting hand. Shoulder rests come in many styles and sizes, so try a few before deciding which one to buy.

Most players favor a standard curvature of the top of the violin bridge. However, it is not uncommon for some players to flatten that arc to facilitate double stops. Again, your own preference will evolve with investigation.

A good bow can cost as much as the whole fiddle. When you are beginning to play, an inexpensive fiberglass bow is sufficient, but after a time, you may want to invest in a good wooden bow. The best of these are made of Pernambuco. In general, wooden bows have a superior combination of balance, strength, and lightness.

Look down the shaft of any bow you plan to buy. With the hair tightened, it should be straight—that is, it should not warp to the right or left. When viewed from the side, however, the stick should curve downward toward the hair. Eventually, the hair of a bow will begin to break. If you have a good stick, it should be rehaired before one quarter of the hair has fallen out. Otherwise, the uneven tension of the hair may warp the bow.

Further Study

There is a lot of great music you can play with only the information supplied in this book—ranging from a fiddle tune to a Bach violin piece. Still, there are eight more major scales (and a few minor variations) that you might encounter as you explore new violin music. For example, jazz players have to be familiar with keys with flats in their signature, because the piano and various horns favor these keys. You'll find it easy to explore these keys on your own because all major scales follow the same step pattern: whole step, whole step, half step, whole step, whole step, whole step, half step.

There will be times when you will need to shift your hand up the neck of the instrument—either to play a high note or to play a double stop that is impossible in a lower position. Bluegrass soloists are increasingly inclined to employ this technique.

Some music seems to sound better when *vibrato* is added. This narrow, controlled shaking of a note was conceived as an imitation of the vibrato of the human voice. Because this device is sometimes employed to mask sour notes, you should be sure you are able to play consistently in tune before adding any vibrato.

Here are some books that you may find useful to further your study of traditional fiddle music.

• *Beginning Old Time Fiddle* by Alan Kaufman (Mr. Kaufman's work inspired the use of finger spacing patterns in this book.)

• *Bluegrass Fiddle Styles* by Kenny Kosek and Stacy Phillips

• *Contest Fiddling* by Stacy Phillips (This book examines Texas-style fiddling, and is available directly from me at 36 Cromwell Hill Road, Monroe, New York 10950.)

Do not play tentatively. Players who are over-cautious about hitting a wrong note take a long time to develop a free-flowing and confident playing style. This does not mean you should concentrate on playing loudly, or particularly fast—just learn to play through your mistakes and get back in the groove without dropping a beat.

Feel free to try fiddling techniques that may be just out of your reach. Experiment with any sound that seems special or appealing. In short, anything that keeps the instrument in your hands and incites you to play with concentration is worthy of your experimentation.

The player's concentration is key to good fiddling.

Appendix: Introduction to Music Notation

Pitches are tones indicated by notes, which appear either on or between the lines of the *staff.*

D   E   F   G   A   B   C   D   E   F   G

When notes above or below the staff are required, *leger lines* are used.

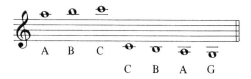

A   B   C

C   B   A   G

The symbol at the beginning of the staff is the *treble clef* (or *G clef,* since it circles the line on which a G note is written).

Most of the music in this book is in $\frac{4}{4}$ *meter,* that is, four beats per measure (indicated by the top number), with each beat lasting the time value of one quarter-note (indicated by the bottom number).

Many fiddle tunes employ $\frac{3}{4}$ *meter,* or *waltz time.* This timing features three beats in each measure, with a quarter note value for each beat.

You'll find it helpful to tap your foot as you play to keep count of the beats. There are four taps to a measure in $\frac{4}{4}$ time. A half note sounds for two taps and a whole note for four.

quarter notes   half notes   whole note

Measures are separated by *barlines.* The end of a section of a tune is denoted by a *double barline.*

A sharp sign ($\sharp$) indicates that a note is raised in pitch by one half-step. A flat sign ($\flat$) indicates that a note is lowered by one half-step. Sharps and flats are collectively known as *accidentals.* These affect all notes of the same pitch occurring within the same measure, unless cancelled by a *natural sign* ($\natural$). Thus, in the example that follows, the second E note is flatted, but the second C note is not sharped.

A quarter note can be subdivided into two eighth notes.

To count an eighth-note rhythm, divide your foot taps into foot-on-the-floor beats and foot-in-the-air offbeats, as indicated.

down	up	down	up	down	up	down	up
1	and	2	and	3	and	4	and

When a note is *dotted,* the time that the note is held is lengthened by half its original value. For example, a *dotted half note* is held for the duration of a half note, plus one quarter note (that is, three beats).

3 beats   2 beats 1 beat

A curved line or *slur* over a group of notes signifies that the bow should not change direction as you play them. Thus, the first four notes in the example that follows should be played with one bowstroke. The next two notes should then be played with one more stroke, and the last two with separate strokes.

A double bar with two dots in front of it is a *repeat sign.* This indicates that you should go back to where you see the inverted repeat sign and play the passage once more. If there is no inverted repeat sign, go back to the beginning of the tune and repeat the passage.

When a passage has a different ending the second time around, the following notation is used.

The bracketed bar marked with the numeral two is called the *second ending,* the bracketed bar marked with a numeral one should be played the first time through. When the passage is repeated, skip the first ending and use the second ending to finish the piece.

The capital letters that occasionally appear over the staff indicate the appropriate chords to be played by a pianist or guitarist as accompaniment. If you can rustle up someone to back up your melodies in this way, you are sure to find new levels of enjoyment. Sharing these wonderful tunes with other musicians is not only good for you, it's great fun.